The Buses of Dumfries and Gal'

in colour photographs by John Sinclair

John Sinclair

The operating territory of the Caledonian extended from Carlisle in the south east to Stranraer depot in the west with its sub depots at Wigtown and Whithorn, and out stations at Newton Stewart and Port William. With very basic premises at the two sub depots, Caledonian had drawn up plans after the war to construct a depot at Newton Stewart. A site near the bus stance had been purchased, but planning permission was refused and the plot was sold in 1955. After Western took over, double deckers were introduced west of Kirkcudbright, and by 1961, there was one each allocated to Whithorn, Newton Stewart and Port William, with five at Stranraer itself. The Port William sleeper was positioned to take school children from the fishing village and surrounding communities to Newton Stewart High School, near where the regular vehicle BAG74 (DC276) was photographed in September 1962. One of 49 AEC Regals with 36 seat Burlingham bodies new in 1946 to Western and its associated companies, it was one of twelve re-bodied in 1955 as double deckers with bodies constructed at Irthlingborough by Bristol Bodyworks to ECW design. One of eight reallocated to the Dumfries area, it was transferred to Stranraer in 1961, and withdrawn in December 1962 when it was sold to the contractor Costain.

© John Sinclair, 2017
First published in the United Kingdom, 2017,
by Stenlake Publishing Ltd.
www.stenlake.co.uk
ISBN 9781840337730

Printed bt Berforts, 17 Burgess Road, Hastings, TN35 4NR

Leith of Sanquhar's unique hybrid Crossley with the body of a pre-war ex-Alexander Leyland Cheetah grafted onto its cab.

Facing page: In 1922, James Gibson introduced a bus service between Moffat and Dumfries, operating from his home in the nearby village of St. Anns. This continued until 1999 from when the company concentrated on private hire and coach tours until closing down in 2007. Caledonian had briefly operated a competing service in the early thirties with a vehicle outstationed at Moffat, but gave up in favour of Gibson. With in addition, a daily service to Ae village and a Wednesday only route from Dumfries to Johnstone Bridge, the fleet in 1962 consisted of two double deckers and four single deckers, two of which were Albions KSM566 and 655 new in 1950 with Scottish Aviation bodies. The former, photographed in Moffat in October 1963, was a CX9 model with a 35 seat body which gave thirteen years of service. One of 27 similar vehicles which emerged from their workshops at Prestwick Airport with light alloy bodies, Scottish Aviation supplied these to Albion Motors on a sub-contract basis for sale to a wide variety of independent operators across the UK.

Introduction

1948 was the first year in which we had a family holiday in Lendalfoot. The Ayrshire coast seemed rather bleak to a seven year old, and the stony beach somewhat uninviting. The chalets were colourful and no two were the same, and the buses passing through every two hours likewise. They were in fact modern vehicles, being utility Guy Arabs with Gardner 6LW engines, each with an individual tuneful growl which appealed to the juvenile ear. With a variety of bodies, rebuilt to varying degrees, and in one case already re-bodied, they had an assortment of adverts. I soon learnt to identify them individually, and recognised that the same buses tended to appear at the same time every day. The roads around the village were tortuous with sharp bends and steep gradients, and I would look for any excuse to travel to nearby Girvan with its Western SMT bus depot.

However, the journey up from my home in Driffield in Yorkshire took us through Carlisle and Dumfries, where I was puzzled by the procession of elderly buses painted in a different shade of red, and with 'Caledonian' on the side. Eventually, I persuaded my uncle who lived in Kilmarnock to take me down to Stranraer to see these vehicles in service and visit the bus depot there, and I began to realise what a fascinating area this was for public transport. Accustomed as I was to visiting Kilmarnock depot, the headquarters of Western, and wandering around the various workshops at a time when relaxed informality was the culture, I was soon to extend my area of interest to cover the south west of Scotland.

In 1953 my family moved to Edinburgh and over the next few years I started travelling independently around the country, initially by public transport, and from 1958 usually hitch hiking. I soon developed a technique whereby I could confidently travel from Edinburgh to youth hostels at Gatehouse of Fleet, Stranraer or Carlisle in the course of a day making it easy to visit Dumfries and Galloway over a weekend. By 1966 I had a car, and it was then possible to cover the entire area in a day, collecting information about the buses and their operation.

However, my main interest had always been to capture on camera the history of bus transport in this area, a part of Scotland traditionally 'off the beaten track.' By 1956 I had acquired my first camera and in 1961 I started to use colour film, taking the first of what has developed into a collection of probably about 250,000 slides of buses throughout the UK. This book simply contains a representative selection of those taken mainly in the 1960s in order to show the variety of vehicles and operators still to be seen in Dumfries and Galloway at that time. Garry Ward's superb book on *Caledonian And Beyond* will give the reader a much greater insight into the history of bus transport throughout the area from the formation of The Caledonian Omnibus Company in 1927 right through to 'deregulation' in 1986 and beyond.

All except one of the Gibson fleet are lined up on the Whitesands in Dumfries in May 1965, the missing vehicle being CCK633 an ex Ribble all Leyland PD2. The other Albion with a Scottish Aviation body was KSM655, a FT39N model with a 31 seat body which was sold the following year to the contractor Carmichael in Lochgilphead. Parked beside it is a further Albion LVA872, a Victor FT39ALF with a Duple 35 seat body, acquired from Hutchison of Overtown in 1961 when only six years old, and withdrawn in 1967. Also acquired from Hutchison was Alexander bodied Leyland Tiger Cub LVD263, new as dealer stock in 1955 with 41 coach seats. Two years later, it was sold to Gibson which operated it as a 45 seat service bus for ten years. Passing on to Mitchell of Luthermuir which was taken over by Alexander Northern in October 1967, it ran for a further five years as their NPD15. The other two double deckers are all Leyland, PD2 demonstrator LTA747 first licensed to Devon General which ran for sixteen years, and ex Wallasey Corporation Metro Cammell bodied PD1 HF9576 acquired in March 1959 and withdrawn seven years later.

Another Dumfriesshire independent to escape acquisition by Caledonian was John Carruthers of New Abbey, who started operating buses from the Solway village of New Abbey into Dumfries in 1921. This service continued to be operated by the Carruthers family until the business was sold to Peacock, a truck operator from Locharbriggs, in December 1983. Caledonian had inherited the service from J&J Scott, which was one of the five constituent companies when it was formed in 1927, running from Dumfries to Southwick via New Abbey, but soon abandoned it in favour of the incumbent operator. The Carruthers family operated a very varied fleet over the years, and two unusual double deckers were photographed in 1962. CCK636 was unique in the Ribble fleet, being the only Leyland PD2 with a Burlingham body not to 'White Lady' status. It was exhibited at the 1948 Commercial Motor Show entering service as Ribble 2648, and withdrawn in May 1960 after swapping engines with a PD1. Acquired from Millburn Motors in August, it ran until November 1964, being sold to the contractor Whatling who operated it for a further three years. AEC Regent III JKM103 was interesting in that, when new in 1947 to Maidstone and District, it was fitted with a five year old Weymann body previously on a 1934 AEC. Acquired in 1958, Carruthers operated it for six years, an unusually long time for an acquired double decker.

By contrast, another long-lived Dumfriesshire independent, Clark of Glencaple, whose services did not compete with the Caledonian, survived until 1965, when the business was sold to Western SMT. Introducing his first motor bus in 1912, James Clark was joined by his sons in 1925, to provide a service from the village of Glencaple on the River Nith to Dumfries. Later operating to Shawhead, further services from Dumfries to Caerlaverock were taken over from R&A Craik in 1944. Caledonian had considered further expansion of its territory in 1936 and Clark's tours which radiated from Dumfries was providing competition. However, no approach was made, and Clark continued with a varied programme of excursions, opening up an office just opposite the bus station. In 'evergreen' colours, compared to the green of the MacGregor tartan, the fleet in July 1963 is lined up at the Whitesands. All Leyland PD1 CTH826 was new in 1946 to James of Ammanford who sold it in 1960 shortly before his business was acquired by South Wales Transport. Five years later Clark sold it to the dealer T.Carruthers in Carrutherstown for use as an office. Roe bodied PD1 EN8540 entered service in March 1946 with Bury Corporation and ran for Clark from May 1959 for six years.

It was, however, the vehicles of Western SMT which occupied most of the extensive area on the Whitesands where buses were parked, sometimes for much of the day in between departures. It was not until late 1991 that a formal bus station was constructed. This view from September 1962 shows a typical line up with Bristol Lodekka LD6G HSD15-16 (DB1227-8) just transferred from Johnstone, one of the two FLF6Gs TCS159-60 (DB1711-2) new in June, and ex Caledonian K6Bs HSM642-3 (DB876-7) with nine months left before withdrawal. The Guy with a highbridge Northern Counties body is one of the three remaining ex Youngs vehicles from the batch XS5650-9/5709 (DY2140-50) with Gardner 6LW engines, transferred from Johnstone in 1958 specifically for use on the Dumfries town services. Of the AECs, BAG88 (DC290) was new in 1946 with a 36 seat Burlingham body, and re-bodied as a double decker by Bristol Bodyworks to Eastern Coach Works design in 1955. Allocated to Kirkcudbright depot for the Dumfries service, it was withdrawn in July 1963. The remaining two are from the batch of thirty with Northern Counties bodies (BAG124-153) 310-39 of which seven were still allocated to the Dumfries area, six at Carlisle and one (331) at Penpont depot. However, all were off by the end of the year.

The first new double deckers in the Caledonian fleet were standard Tilling group Bristols with Eastern Coachworks 55 seat bodies HSM642-3 (323-4) which became DB876-7 when the company was taken over by Western SMT in January 1950. New in October 1948 as K6Bs they were the first Bristol engined vehicles in the fleet, and with the others from this order HSM644-5 (325-6) which appeared in February 1950, were the only Bristol K class delivered to an operator north of the border. Initially they were used on the service from Dumfries to Sanquhar where one was garaged overnight at the premises of motor engineer Peter Turnbull. When this route was extended through to Ayr after the Caledonian and Western services were linked up, it was kept at Western's premises in Queens Road. Photographed in April 1963, DB876 has arrived in from Castle Douglas where it is garaged overnight for the 6.45 am service to Dumfries via Kirkpatrick Durham. With DB877, it was withdrawn in June, thus surviving three years longer than the batch of ten Bristol L5Gs only a year older. Caledonian had little need for new double deckers at that time as all the elderly Leyland Titans had been extensively rebuilt or re-bodied during or after the war, with the eight receiving new Croft bodies in 1947 being effectively new vehicles. Most already had their petrol engines replaced by diesel units. Two of these used on the Dumfries to Edinburgh service were allocated to the Edinburgh depot at Hayfield in Gorgie Road, where up to ten vehicles were garaged at that time.

HSM644-5 (DB878-9) were Bristol K5G chassis and never ran for Caledonian, being diverted to London Transport which had a vehicle shortage, but didn't want Bristol engined vehicles. With Tilling style destination boxes they were eminently suitable, although they eventually ended up with the standard Western display at that time incorporating an illuminated 'Western' panel as shown by DB878 parked at the Whitesands in July 1963, a month before withdrawal. The pair were allocated to Annan depot by 1956, operating local services and into Carlisle spending every alternate night there, and on Saturday running duplicates to Dumfries via the 'High Road.' Four similar vehicles were on order at the time of the takeover, but were diverted to other members of the Tilling group. All of DB876-9 saw further service with TD Alexander (Greyhound) of Sheffield and Arbroath, numbered 83-6 with the last pair initially running at Arbroath, 86 not being transferred down until May 1965.

In the same month as the last of the former Caledonian vehicles were withdrawn, the first of Western's 36 feet long buses entered service at Dumfries as VCS391-8 (DL1837-44.) These were Leyland Leopards with 49 seat Alexander bodies to the newly-introduced Y type design, which Western continued to buy for another seventeen years. However, all subsequent orders were for the 'dual purpose' wide bay version until 1975. With leathercloth seats and fluorescent lights they provided a degree of comfort for passengers on the Stranraer to Dumfries and Dumfries to Carlisle services replacing three year old 41 seat Bristol MW6Gs with Alexander 41 seat bodies. Ten years previously, Western was using a mixture of pre-war Dennis Lancets and Bristol L5Gs of varying ages on their flagship service between Dumfries and Carlisle, and I well remember an article in *The Sunday Post* where passengers complained about the 'twenty year old' buses that appeared on this route. With the exception of one further Leopard in 1968, KCS150F (DL2179) this batch were the last new vehicles allocated to Dumfries until similar WSD747-50K (DL2357-60) appeared in 1972, apart from three Daimler Fleetlines UCS289-91K (DR2291-3) in 1971. DL1842 was photographed on the Whitesands in July 1963 on the 47 service to Carlisle, although the official allocation was 1837 at Carlisle, 1838-9 at Annan and 1840 at Dumfries for the Carlisle service, and 1843-4 at Stranraer with 1841-2 at Dumfries for the Stranraer service.

The entire batch of 1963 Leopards remained allocated to the Dumfries area until withdrawn in 1979, although 1840 spent the last year of its life at Kilmarnock. SL1844 remained at Stranraer, acquiring the depot code 'S' when the sub depots at Stranraer(S) and Carlisle (E) were given their own codes in June 1977. It is now in the standard livery with the skirt panel red and converted for OMO operation with a power operated door. It was withdrawn in June 1979, later operating with Dack of Terrington St. Clement. Photographed at Newton Stewart bus station in September 1977, it is officially allocated to Stranraer's own sub depot at Whithorn, operating the feeder service (70) from Isle of Whithorn to Newton Stewart. Connecting with it is OSJ630R (SL2630) outstationed there, and one of five (2626-30) 53 seat Leopards with long bay bodies allocated new to Stranraer in 1976. On the 59 service, it has returned from Girvan taking school children from the Academy to the villages of Pinwherry and Barrhill. The implementation of one man only operation had been completed at Stranraer earlier in the year, and the 59 service became fully OMO in January 1978.

Five years earlier in 1972, the scene at Newton Stewart is different. The vehicle returning to Isle of Whithorn is MSD418 (DG1554) one of nine (1548-56) Guy LUFs with Alexander bodies identical to the Bristol MW6Gs, which were allocated new to the Dumfries area in 1960 and remained until withdrawn between 1975 and 1977. They were in fact the last Guys delivered to a UK operator. DG1554 spent its entire life at Stranraer depot, being converted for OMO operation in July 1965, although there is only a windscreen sticker to indicate this. However, the alteration included fitting a manual door control linkage to the one piece door, and rear reversing lights. It was withdrawn in August 1975 and scrapped. Connecting with it is the coach on the 3 3/4 hour journey from Stranraer to Dumfries, DSD713D (DT2072) one of four (2070-3) Bristol RELH6Gs with 38 seats and toilets new for the London service, transferred to Dumfries for duplication in December 1969. They were from a batch of 21 (2060-79/2184) which apart from one only briefly (2063 burnt out) eventually all ended up in the Dumfries area, including the pair (2060-1) transferred to Highland Omnibuses. They had a complex history, and 2072-3 were converted in September 1971 to 45 non reclining seats without toilets, and their one piece doors altered to air operation for OMO work. In 1976 they were repainted into red and cream livery, running for another four years.

Back in 1962, the buses at Newton Stewart were parked up on open ground, and the 'sleeper' for the Glasgow service was an Ayr based vehicle, here Leyland PD3 RCS385 (AD1687) awaiting to return, but displaying the route number (03) for the Stranraer to Glasgow service. Route numbers were not in fact introduced until 1956 and did not appear in the timetables until 1957. New in 1961, it operated from Ayr all its life until withdrawn in 1977. From August 1972 this duty came under the control of Stranraer depot when Leopard CAG438C was transferred from Ayr. This service had originally started from Ayr, shortened to operate from Girvan to Newton Stewart during the war and was traditionally operated by a single decker, Leyland TS8 AAG114 being the regular vehicle at that time. By 1950, double deckers were used, and Girvan depot's contribution by then was Guy Arab ASD413. Parked beside the PD3 is RAG411 (DB1645), one of four Bristol LD6Gs with platform doors (1644-7) also new to Stranraer depot in 1961, being its first new double deckers ever, and first with platform doors. They spent their entire lives based at Stranraer until withdrawn in 1976/7. As the Stranraer 'sleeper' at Newton Stewart, it is required for the 6 am service from the railway station to Isle of Whithorn, returning to the High School and the station at 8.50. The railway line from Stranraer to Dumfries closed in June 1965, but this extension from Dashwood Square to the station continued for two more years. Bristol MW6G OCS714 (DT1592) parked off a school contract from Whithorn depot was one of two (1592-3) new to Stranraer depot in 1960 for the Dumfries service and converted for OMO operation in 1965, remaining there until withdrawn in 1976.

The 85 mile journey between Stranraer and Glasgow (03) was the longest service in Britain to be operated by double deckers in the 1960s, and when Ayr depot received 27 new Leyland PD3s (AD1671-97) in 1961, they were immediately allocated to this route, and also the other long distance services from Glasgow to Newton Stewart (059) and Castle Douglas (051). The schedules ensured that only buses from Ayr depot, rather than Newton Mearns which supplied vehicles from the Glasgow end, were outstationed at the southern termini overnight, and this historical arrangement continued until 1972 when 1671 was transferred to Stranraer depot for the 03 service, becoming DD1671. Ironically, it was withdrawn in June 1977, the very month the 'S' code was introduced for the Stranraer allocation, although a Leopard was allocated to this service from 1973. The last ten had bodies by Northern Counties, but this photograph taken in 1963 in Lendalfoot where I spent childhood holidays, shows an Alexander bodied example heading for Girvan, passing the well where we obtained our drinking water. No corresponding bus was transferred from Ayr depot to compensate for the Castle Douglas sleeper being provided by Kirkcudbright depot. While the road curves gently here, some sections of the road were tortuous, and I well remember as a child seeing a newspaper cutting of a highbridge Northern Counties bodied Guy, BAG387, mimicking *The Italian Job*, suspended over a high drop on to the beach near Cairn Ryan after sliding on the ice.

Girvan depot had always historically supplied vehicles for the Stranraer to Glasgow service, and surprisingly these were double deckers even in 1948 when I first visited Lendalfoot. Utility Guy Arabs with the more powerful Gardner 6LW engine, these included distinctive and unique vehicles such as ASD409, 410 and 253, replaced from 1950 by Albion Venturers with powerful and silent 9.9 litre engines. The service had been truncated to operate just from Stranraer to Ayr due to wartime restrictions, but through operation to Glasgow resumed in 1949. Over the years successive batches of buses at Ayr were officially allocated to Girvan sub depot, with a varied selection of about 16 vehicles, historically double deckers but when 44 seat Guy LUFs with Alexander bodies were briefly allocated to the Stranraer service in 1955, three of the six at Ayr depot were based at Girvan GCS195-6/8 (AG1110-1/3.) Older buses were stationed there for the frequent services to Ayr via Kirkoswald, Dailly and Maidens, and three Leyland PD2/20s with Northern Counties bodies KAG823-5 (AD1342-4) operated on these routes during 1971 before moving to Johnstone depot when Girvan introduced one man only operation in June 1972. AD1343 was new in June 1957, one of five of the seven vehicles in a batch of 37 which had platform doors allocated to Ayr for the premium 04 route to Glasgow and withdrawn exactly 20 years later.

However, the vehicles long associated with the services from Girvan to Ayr were the last batch of Guy Arab IVs bought new by Western SMT JCS4-10/429-34 (Y1247-59) with as usual Gardner 6LW engines, this time Alexander 59 seat bodies, which entered service in October 1956. Ayr depot received 1247-56 with platform doors, and also 1257 without. Initially used on the 04 and 03 routes, 1247-53 were officially allocated to Girvan depot in 1961 to replace the Alexander bodied Albion Venturers associated with the depot since new in late 1949. 1254-7 followed two years later when ESD208-11 (AY1010-3) Western's first Arab IVs (with Northern Counties bodies) moved to the parent depot. When new in 1953, they had been confined to the Glasgow to Ayr via Troon route as being eight feet wide could not use the Waterloo St bus station in Glasgow. Later, when the bays were widened, they were able to operate the 03 route. Similar DY1014-6, Dumfries depot's first new double deckers had been allocated to the Stranraer to Dumfries service, but in both cases, they had been superseded by the infamous Guys LUFs with their semi high but hard 44 seats. The entire batch remained at Girvan until 1967 when 1247/56 moved down to Dumfries, and 1248 up to Greenock, together with 1257 which joined the other two there without doors. The remainder were withdrawn in 1971 and replaced by Leyland Leopards. 1251/4-5/7 were photographed in the depot yard in April 1963.

Despite those with platform doors being 15 years old, only one of the batch of 1956 Guy Arabs (1259) never found another operator, eventually ending up in a scrapyard at Carlton near Barnsley. All the rest, after being sold to various dealers, ran for other operators throughout Scotland, and one (1256) went to an operator in Yorkshire, Johnson of Wyke, near Bradford. Interestingly, 1247 (JCS4) which moved from Girvan to Carlisle depot in 1967, then Stranraer in 1969, had a peripatetic afterlife, being withdrawn in June 1971 and sold to the dealer, Millburn Motors, in Glasgow. In July it appeared with my local operator, Allander of Milngavie, still in Western's colours, but was returned to S&N (dealers) the successor to Millburn Motors in May 1972. A month later it was sold to Carruthers of New Abbey, fleet number 8, when I photographed it on the Whitesands, freshly painted. However, a year later it returned to S&N, moving on to T.D. Alexander (Greyhound) of Arbroath who operated it for a further four years. A previous ex Western Arab IV GSD707 (1186) with a Northern Counties body had also operated for Carruthers for a year, being exchanged at S&N with 1247. Coincidentally, JCS9 (1252) was acquired by nearby operator, Leith of Sanquhar, who ran it for a further two years before it finally ended up with a contractor.

Another Guy Arab which frequented the Whitesands at Dumfries was FTD450, which was the last purchase of Clark of Glencaple, in December 1964. It had started off life with Rawtenstall Corporation (No.37) as a Mark II chassis in September 1943 with a Massey utility body which was replaced by a new East Lancs one in 1951. With a Gardner 6LW engine, it was sold to the dealer Irvine (Tiger Coaches) of Salsburgh in August 1964. However, its life with Clark was short and it was never repainted, passing to Western in August 1965 when it was immediately sold to the dealer Millburn Motors. Beside it is the other bus acquired by Western and immediately sold, FJA612, an all Leyland Royal Tiger new to North Western Road Car Company (no.612) of Stockport in 1953. Acquired by Clark from the dealer Cowley of Salford in September 1962, it passed to McLennan of Spittalfield after Western sold it to Millburn Motors. It was converted in the innovative Spittalfield workshops to front entrance for OMO operation, entering service in April 1966 and running for another six years before being cannibalised.

However, it was the Guys of Western SMT which were very much a feature of the Whitesands in the early 1960s, and a total of 61 operated in the Dumfries area between 1951 and 1971. Of these 29 were utility vehicles of which 21 had been re-bodied, and 24 had previously operated for London Transport. Of the last group, nine had received new Alexander bodies in 1952 (DY999-1007) and immediately dispatched south with 999-1003 allocated to Carlisle depot, 1005-7 to Lockerbie, and 1004 later to Annan. 1002-7 had their Gardner 5LW engines replaced with the 6LW version, followed by 1000 later. They were withdrawn between 1962 and 1964, with 1004-6 passing to Highland Omnibuses. 1007 (ex LTE G196), new in 1945 with a Park Royal body, was the last of the batch to be withdrawn in March 1964. It was photographed at Annan depot in April 1963, parked behind the garage and adjacent to the station. The original depot had been a converted redundant church, burnt down in 1939 and rebuilt, but modified in 1967 by Western with the construction of a rear door. The allocation of twelve buses had been progressively reduced, until when closed in 1986 there were only two double deckers which were parked on waste ground at the rear of the bingo hall. Parked beside it is Bristol MW6G OCS722 (DT1600) which uniquely was transferred to Thornliebank's remote Argyllshire sub depot at Ardrishaig in 1972, to operate the ex MacBrayne service to Oban.

The oldest vehicle operated from Annan depot that day was a 28 year old Leyland Tiger TS7 CS2027 (DL51), new in June 1935, with a problematic metal-framed Leyland body which was replaced three years later. Photographed at the Whitesands, it was waiting to return on a part service duplicate to its home town. Western was short of double deckers during the war, and 23 from this batch were re-bodied with Alexander lowbridge bodies. Five survived until 1950 when one received a highbridge Burlingham body, and four (CS2005/21/2/7) were given new all-metal 35 seat Alexander bodies with dual purpose seats. As DL47-9/51 they were immediately sent to Dumfries depot to replace ageing ex Caledonian vehicles, where they remained until 1963 used on service work, but also private hires. Later fitted with Leyland's early post war 7.4 litre engine, they proved to be reliable and indestructible all purpose machines, and all four saw further service with other operators with DL51 last licensed in 1968 to a timber merchant Howie of Dunlop. Interestingly, this firm was involved in the construction of the new depots at Wigtown and Whithorn. A further four TS7 chassis from the 1937 intake were similarly re-bodied and also dispatched to depots of the former Caledonian empire.

All eight of these elderly vehicles, many older than the former Caledonian vehicles which they would replace, tended to stay at the peripheral depots for their entire life, with the four 1937 arrivals remaining at Carlisle. DL47 was allocated to Lockerbie, 48 to Dumfries itself and 49 (CS2022), photographed here at Newton Stewart in 1962, to Stranraer. Originally in the red and cream dual purpose livery, it had recently been repainted into service bus colours, and was parked up for the day, due to return to its home depot of Whithorn on a school contract. Although the Stranraer allocation at that time consisted of eight double deckers and twelve single deckers, only nine remained at the home depot overnight, with a double decker outstationed at both Newton Stewart and Port William. Whithorn depot had one double decker with three single deckers overnight, and Wigtown depot housed five single deckers. The schedules, constructed to allow vehicles to be changed over for fuelling, servicing and the operation of school contracts, were very complex and enabled exchanges with both Stranraer and Dumfries depots. Latterly DL51 tended to operate out of Whithorn depot, and after withdrawal was used by a contractor in Salisbury, being licensed until 1966 when 31 years old.

Further cascading of elderly re-bodied Leyland Tigers down to the Dumfries area occurred during the 1950s, and by 1957 all twenty TS8 'specials' (DL162-81) with Alexander 39 seat dual purpose bodies were scattered throughout Dumfries and Galloway. New in 1939-40, they were the remainder (AAG101-16/20/3-5) of a batch re-bodied with identical bodies in 1950-1, having escaped requisition by the MOD in 1940, although one was ultimately returned in 1949, but never re-bodied. They tended to move around the former Caledonian territory, and DL162-3 were photographed at Whithorn depot in April 1963 during the school holidays when lying spare. The very basic Caledonian garage in Glasserton Street, which did have a fuel tank, had been dismantled in 1955, and the four buses were parked overnight at the old railway station where an office for the depot inspector was rented and the fuel tank relocated. The station was still being used for freight traffic at that time. The following year, the new depot constructed on land leased from the SCWS, was completed, followed by the depot at Wigtown. Now in service bus livery with Leyland 7.4 litre engines, they were near the end of their lives, and 162, recently transferred from Kirkcudbright depot, was withdrawn five months later and sold to a contractor in Belfast. 163 survived a year longer, also ending up with a contractor, like most of the batch.

Only the last four of the re-bodied Leyland TS8s entered service in service bus livery, at Inchinnan depot for the Glasgow to Largs via Renfrew service. Six (DL169-74) were immediately allocated to the Dumfries area in 1951, and being in the red and cream livery were used as weekend extras on the Glasgow to Blackpool service and day tours as well as service work. Although the seats could perhaps be described as dual purpose, the interior fittings which included extras such as coloured light shades were reasonably lavish. Only one (DL174, AAG113) retained these colours to the end, and was photographed in the depot at Dumfries, having arrived in from its home depot of Penpont on 10th April 1963 on the Wednesday service via Burnhead. Withdrawn in June 1964 when 24 years old, it too passed to a contractor, Palmer of Kilwinning. Ultimately only two (167 and 169) of the twenty vehicles did not find a new owner, most passing through the hands of the Glasgow dealer Millburn Motors. Parked behind it is one of the six Leyland PS1s new in 1949 with 35 seat metal-framed Alexander bodies, transferred to Dumfries in 1960-1, which makes an interesting comparison in body styles with there being only a year's difference in age. However, despite the chassis being ten years newer, they only remained in service for an additional year.

The Leyland PS1 chassis was also popular with independents as an economical and reliable model. Second hand purchases from large operators disposing of them prematurely, when underfloor vehicles came available, were popular throughout the country. Carruthers obtained such a machine from East Yorkshire Motor Services via its usual dealer, PVD of Dunchurch, in December 1958. New in July 1948, JAT426 (no.458) had a 30 seat Brush body with a rear entrance, a feature which East Yorkshire had, with rare exceptions, always favoured even for coaches. Surprisingly, it was withdrawn when only eight years old and initially stored. Entering service with Carruthers in May 1959 (no. 10), it operated for nearly eight more years having its seating capacity increased to 33, and was sold to a contractor, Rankin of Sandbank near Dunoon in December 1966. Parked beside it on the Whitesands when it was photographed in July 1963 is Gibson's Leyland Tiger Cub LVD263. The only other PS1 operated by Carruthers was also from East Yorkshire, HAT647 with a similar Weymann body, which only completed ten years in service before disposal. It entered service with Carruthers in June 1958 and ran for five more years before sale to the contractor Cruden of Musselburgh.

Another Dumfriesshire operator to run a couple of Leyland PS1s from a Yorkshire operator was J&J Leith of Sanquhar, who started running buses between Sanquhar and Kirkconnel in 1925, at times jointly with Western SMT. They continued to operate on this service until they ceased bus operation in 1997. They also had a number of contracts to the surrounding mines and, as the local company, operated tours, excursions and private hires. However, their most interesting service was up to Wanlockhead, the highest village in Scotland, and on to Leadhills. A regular vehicle on this service was Mulliner bodied Bedford OB SW7944, new to Davidson of Auchencairn in 1949, and purchased by Leith in 1957 who ran it until 1965. Photographed at Leith's Nithsdale Garage at Sanquhar in July 1965, it is now delicensed and parked beside HD7887. It was one of 75 PS1s new in 1948 to Yorkshire Woollen District (no.604) with 34 seat Brush bodies, of which 24 were converted to double deck specification with Metro-Cammell bodies in 1954-5. First acquired by J.Young of AA Motor Services in 1955, it passed to Leith in September 1963, running until December 1969. HD7875 also came to Leith from AA, but in 1960 and was withdrawn in 1964.

Leith had a very varied fleet with some unusual buses, including a couple of AEC Regals RC9687 and 9693 which were the same age as the Leyland Tigers, but re-bodied after ten years. RC9693 photographed on the same day was new to Trent Motor Traction of Derby (no.787) in 1947 with a 35 seat Willowbrook body. In 1958, with the chassis extended to 30 feet, Willowbrook rebuilt the body with a full front, increasing the seating capacity to 39. Sold to dealer Cowley in Salford, Leith acquired it with RC9687 in September 1963 and operated them both for five years. Parked beside it is DRN280, an all Leyland PD2 new to Ribble Motor Services (no.1340) in December 1950 with hand-operated platform doors, one of 50 similar vehicles withdrawn between 1964 and 1965 which found new owners all over Britain. It also came to Leith via the dealer Cowley, in May1964, and ran for seven years. Interestingly, a similar vehicle (DAG389) but highbridge, acquired from J.Young of AA Motors, had platform doors fitted by Leith before entering service in August 1965.

The most unusual vehicle of all was a new arrival in 1949, a Crossley SD42 with a rare 33 seat Santus body. Apart from a Bedford SB in 1952, this was Leith's only new purchase until 1961. However, the Santus body proved unsatisfactory and remedial work was required, completed in 1962. This entailed grafting the body of a 1938 Leyland Cheetah to the cab and front bulkhead of the Crossley. The resulting hybrid ran for a further five years and was often used on the service to Leadhills, which at that time extended through the Mennock Pass up to Abington three times a day, in order to connect with the Dumfries to Edinburgh service of Scottish Omnibuses. On a Saturday, there were two through runs to Lanark, making a total journey time of an hour and 40 minutes, an arduous journey for ex Birmingham Daimler CWA6 FOP386 which on occasions was required. However, the single return trip on a Sunday evening only required a single decker and KSM40 was often used. The donor vehicle was WG7508, new to Alexander in July 1938 with a 39 seat Alexander body, and acquired in October 1957 through the dealer Millburn Motors.

At the other end of Sanquhar from Leith's premises was Western's depot in Queens Road, and parked beside it in June 1974 is Alexander bodied Albion Lowlander VCS427 (CN1873.) Resting between trips to the local pits, it was one of two parked overnight, together with a Daimler Fleetline operated OMO for the local service to Kirkconnel, and inside the garage, two Leopards, one each for the Ayr and Glasgow services to Dumfries. The capacity of the Fleetline was not required for most of the day, but elderly people preferred the 'low floor' entry. The Lowlander was one of a batch of thirty (1852-81) new in 1963/4, of which four (1868-71) were allocated new to Cumnock depot with 1858/66-7/72-4 being transferred in 1967. Although a standard 69 seat model, it and 1873 were transferred to Stranraer depot in February 1976 and converted for OMO operation for use on school contracts to the local academy from nearby villages such as Glenluce and Kirkcolm. A further three Lowlanders joined them in October, but were not similarly converted, and all five had left Stranraer within four months, replaced by Fleetlines. 1873 was then transferred to Ayr and withdrawn in November 1978, ending up with dealers in Barnsley.

The only other Albion Lowlander to be similarly converted for OMO operation was VCS413 (DN1859) new to Kilmarnock depot in January 1964. A solitary transfer to Dumfries depot in April 1976, it was specifically for the school contract leaving at 7.50am taking children from the village of Dunscore, continuing through Moniaive and Penpont to Wallacehall Academy at 9.15am. Parking up at Penpont depot during the day, it was photographed on Wednesday 9th June 1976 beside Leyland Leopard CAG433C (DL2018) which had returned from the Wednesday service from Penpont to Dumfries via Burnhead. Attached to its front grille is a hand-made, polished aluminium star, a feature introduced by drivers at Penpont depot. This was seen on the radiators of Western buses for many years, and two (BAG146/50) of the four Northern Counties bodied AEC Regents at Penpont in the late 1950s (BAG145-6/8/50) displayed these stars. The other five vehicles parked at Penpont overnight were three more Leopards, 2019-20 and 2453 (RAG394M), and two Bristol MW6Gs, 1649/52 (RCS335/8) which were all on its official allocation at that time of six buses. The conversion of 1859 to OMO operation involved fitting a sliding partition in the window behind the driver, a periscope, an internal mirror and reversing lights. Despite displacing a Daimler Fleetline which had been on this contract since 1973, it was withdrawn in March 1979, and replaced by GCS161E (DR2100.) It was one of two 33 feet long 83 seat Fleetlines new to Paisley depot in 1967 fully converted for OMO operation, which were transferred down for school contracts. The other (SR2099) had a periscope and was used to take children from Glenluce to Stranraer Academy.

Fourteen years previously, the double decker used on the Wallacehall school contract, was also a high capacity vehicle, RAG389 (DB1623), one of only two 70 seat Bristol Lodekka FL6Gs with the Gardner 6LX engine in the Western fleet. New in February 1961, it was immediately allocated to Penpont depot for this contract and I photographed it there in September 1962. The other double decker then at Penpont was a standard LD6G model RAG401 (DB1635) for the service from Moniaive to Dumfries, which was not replaced by a single decker until 1971. The following year DB1623's duty was moved to the parent depot at Dumfries to be operated OMO by a Daimler Fleetline, and it was transferred to Kirkcudbright depot. This marked the end of double deck operation at a rural depot first built by Caledonian in 1935, after it had taken over the business of J Bell of Penpont and a wooden garage in 1932. After the war, consideration was given to relocating the depot two miles eastwards to Thornhill to cater for the main through traffic, but this never took place. As a result of the Market Analysis Project (SCOTMAP) to assess the long-term sustainability of bus services, changes introduced in January 1983 reduced the allocation to two single deckers, and the depot finally closed on 26th October 1968.

DB1623's transfer to Kirkcudbright depot was again to operate a school run which required a high capacity double decker for the 7.55 service from Dalbeattie to Kirkcudbright High School via Auchencairn. The duty was constructed as a circular route leaving the parent depot at 7.05 am reaching Dalbeattie via Castle Douglas, and had previously been operated by 60 seater Lodekka DB1643. However, in September 1976, with the depot converted to OMO operation, it was replaced by a 53 seat Leopard, and sent to a local dealer for scrap in December. The other Bristol, FL6G DB1624, had also worked at Kirkcudbright between 1962 and 1971 on a school service from Ringford and Twynholm into Kirkcudbright, but when replaced by the smaller DB1643 was transferred up to Johnstone depot for more intensive use on services to Glasgow and Largs. Withdrawn in February 1977, it was converted into a Tow Wagon for Highland Omnibuses. However, Dumfries also employed the pair on busy services, particularly the local service from Lincluden to Locharbriggs on Saturdays and during the school holidays, and from Dumfries to Gatehouse of Fleet on summer Saturdays.

There had been a depot at Kirkcudbright since the formation of Caledonian in 1927 when it inherited the wooden building of the Brooks Motor Company. While modernised over the years, it was not until 1957 that Western constructed the harbour garage which could accommodate double deckers, and in that year the allocation consisted of AEC double deckers BAG142-3 with Northern Counties bodies and BAG88 re-bodied by Bristol, and 39 seat Leyland TS8s AAG101/6-7. At its maximum in 1978, there were twelve OMO single deckers, with two parked overnight in Dalbeattie station yard until 1980, reduced after SCOTMAP in 1983 to only five. Officially closed in 1986, Western rented space until 1989, when the remaining two were just parked outside. From June 1972, the Castle Douglas to Ayr duty had come under the control of Dumfries depot, and the single decker kept at Market Hill car park was moved to Kirkcudbright. Officially Leopard CAG466C (DL2051) it alternated night about with an Ayr depot Leopard. Although never formally allocated there, Leopards DDB161-4C (DL2660-3) new to North Western (no.161-4) arrived at Dumfries in 1977, and with twin speed back axles were very popular in the area for the next three years. In May 1978, Dalbeattie sleeper DL2660 has arrived via the coast duplicated by 2661 from Auchencairn.

Stranraer depot however remains to this day in Lewis Street, where Caledonian constructed a new depot in 1935 designed to allow the garaging of lorries and buses. There was also a small rented office at the bus stance at Port Rodie which was finally vacated in 1981. The allocation had risen to 34 buses in 1972, consisting of eleven Bristol Lodekkas, DD1671 for the Glasgow run, nine 49 seat Leopards, two Bristol REs off the London service, and eleven 41 seat Guy LUFs and Bristol MW6Gs. Of these, Whithorn depot had three Lodekkas and two 41 seaters, Port William one Lodekka, Newton Stewart one 49 seater and Wigtown three 41 seaters, with the remainder at the parent depot. This photograph taken in June that year shows the half of the depot used for buses with one of the former London coaches (DT2073-4) inside. At the entrance is OCS715 (DT1593) the other Bristol MW6G allocated new to Stranraer depot, waiting to leave for Portpatrick. It was transferred out to Lockerbie in 1975, and sold to Davidson of Forfar in August 1976. Parked outside is RAG407 (DB1641) one of 20 Bristol LD6G (1628-47) allocated new to the Dumfries area in 1961 and just transferred to Stranraer. It moved on to Carlisle in 1975, was sold in June 1976 and exported to the USA. The destination Wig Bay was used for contracts to the holiday park on the shore of Loch Ryan.

The type of Stranraer vehicle outstationed at the four locations was determined mainly by the number of children attending Newton Stewart High School from the various communities.In September 1962, the double decker at Whithorn depot, RAG410 (DB1644) (although RAG411 was the official allocation) when Caledonian started the day with a run from Port William via Isle of Whithorn to take primary school children into Whithorn, whereupon it would operate the 9.25 68 service along Luce Bay and via Auchenmalg to Stranraer. While busy on a Friday, this service demanded a double decker on a Saturday and on summer Sundays. As the years passed by, passenger numbers dwindled and after SCOTMAP's recommendations, the service which had been started in 1925 by one of the founding directors of Caledonian was finally withdrawn in January 1983. A more interesting service that could be operated by a double decker was the Whithorn 'express' to Glasgow on the third Wednesday of each month, which actually picked up at road ends as well as villages on the way to Newton Stewart, and thence via Girvan to Glasgow. Departing at 7am, the journey took 4hrs15mins, arriving back at Whithorn at 10.45pm. Introduced in 1952, it was sometimes operated by Leyland TD1s over 20 years old such as HD4363, but usually a 41 seater by the 1960s, and was finally withdrawn in 1971. DB1644 remained at Stranraer depot until withdrawn in November 1976, being exported to Keswick in Ontario.

All the Lodekkas allocated to the Stranraer area over the years had platform doors. The entire batch of Western's first Lodekkas (GCS237-256) B1151-70 new in 1955 were given a baptism of fire when allocated to Greenock depot and its hilly terrain. They were subsequently moved down to the Dumfries area in three batches between 1962 and 1964, and 1167-70 were later fitted with platform doors at Dumfries using kits supplied by Eastern Coach Works. DB1169-70 arrived at Stranraer in July 1963 and were converted in October 1966 when they also lost the illuminated panel which originally displayed 'Local' above the destination screen. This had been replaced in 1960 when at Greenock depot with the word 'Western.' Although the batch had been delivered with full length radiator grilles, all apart from 1167 later acquired the shorter style which was standard on all subsequent orders. The pair remained at Stranraer until withdrawn in April 1975 and were converted to Tow Wagons at Dumfries, 1169 becoming KW7045 at Kilmarnock depot continuing until 1980. 1167 (and 1168 later transferred to Stranraer) also survived until then, four years longer than the rest of the batch. 1169 was photographed near Lochans en route from Portpatrick to Stranraer in June 1972, a service operated by Caledonian from its formation in 1927.

The first new vehicles to be allocated to the Dumfries area were in fact Guy Arab UFs EAG472-5 (DG970-3) in 1952, with centre entrance 'Coronation Coach' Alexander bodies, often referred to as the 'bombers.' DG971-2 had 36 seats, but the following year were converted to 30 seat coaches with toilets for use on the Glasgow to London service. DG970 and 973 retained their 41 seats, and all four remained in the area in black and white coach colours until transferred to Highland Omnibuses in 1963 (971-2) and 1965 (970/3.) However 970/3 spent the last year of their life with Western at Stranraer depot on routine service work, and DG973 was photographed at the bus stance at Port Rodie in September 1964 awaiting to depart on the Saturday only 9.30 am service to the village of Auchenree. Surprisingly, the office premises at the bus stance were somewhat basic. This service originally ran through to Portpatrick, but was truncated to operate only to Auchenree in 1957, and withdrawn in 1970. EAG475 arrived in Inverness in December 1965, having been painted into Highland's red and cream service bus livery in Kilmarnock, and operated out of Inverness depot on both local and long distance services, as was Highland's custom, until withdrawn in August 1967 and sold for scrap. Parked behind it at Port Rodie is Stranraer's Leopard, VCS397 (DL1845), awaiting to depart on the 10.05 service to Dumfries.

Another Guy single decker to end up in the fleet of Highland Omnibuses was GCS207 (DG1122) one of the sixteen LUFs (1110-25) new in 1955 with 44 seat Alexander bodies. Introduced with publicity to provide modern, comfortable and fast vehicles for Western's trunk services, they were uncomfortable and not successful and replaced. On the Glasgow to Stranraer and Dumfries routes this was by double deckers once again. The Stranraer to Dumfries service however continued with single deckers, but with 41 seat dual purpose versions of the Alexander body. DG1116-25 were the first new service buses to appear in the former Caledonian area, and were allocated as 1117-8 to Stranraer depot for the Dumfries service, 1123-4 to Annan and 1125 to Carlisle for the Carlisle to Dumfries service (initially running through to Glasgow) and the rest to the parent depot. All left in 1959, but 1110-4/7/21-5 were reallocated to Dumfries later, and 1110-24 all transferred to Highland Omnibuses in 1968. DG1122 initially used on the Glasgow to Carlisle service, moved to Greenock in 1959 and returned in May 1965, sporting an additional front grille. It was photographed at the Whitesands in July 1967, ironically on loan to Stranraer depot and operating the trunk service to Dumfries. In May 1968 it moved up to Nairn depot as Highland GL23 for service work into Inverness, later a school bus at Dornoch, but was never repainted and withdrawn for scrap in May 1971. It retained its one piece manually operated door to the end, and was never converted for OMO operation.

A futher batch of Lodekkas were cascaded down to the Dumfries area, this time all but one of Johnstone's allocation of seventeen of the next batch of Lodekkas (HSD15-34) B1227-46 new in 1956, again in three batches between 1962 and 1964. DB1227-37/41-5 were also subsequently fitted with platform doors, but only survived until 1972-3 with GB1238-40/6 at Greenock depot only reaching 1970. The later vehicles in this batch (1232-46) were fitted with the triangular 'Scottish Bus Group' destination arrangement, first introduced by Western in January of that year on a batch of Northern Counties bodied Leyland PD2/20s when route numbers were introduced. This photograph taken at Annan depot in July 1968 shows the contrasting destination screens on 1228 and 1235, 1228 being parked up from Carlisle depot off a school run from Gretna to Annan Academy. RAG399 (DB1633) was delivered new to Annan depot, its first ever new double decker, and remained until the depot was fully OMO operational on 4th December 1976. It was withdrawn in March 1977 and acquired by a circus. LCS208 (DT1398) had just arrived from Johnstone depot, and with a two piece folding door had been converted for OMO operation to join 1404, and 1704/9 already at Annan. Withdrawn in April 1975, it was sold to Inveresk medical research unit for staff transport. One of twenty Bristol MW6Gs (1387-1406) with Alexander dual purpose bodies, these vehicles were the first single deckers at Dumfries to have a separate screen for route numbers when 1395 and 1400 arrived in 1959.

Carlisle depot had an allocation of seventeen double deckers and twelve single deckers when this picture of Longtown depot was taken in March 1964. However, accommodation was limited in the combined bus station and depot, and 3 D/D with 3 S/Ds were parked at Longtown overnight, 3 S/Ds in Gretna garage and one S/D at Langholm. A garage at Longtown had been acquired by Caledonian with the business of Lochinvar Motor Services in 1939 and with double deckers being acquired from 1938 onwards, they were outstationed there. The depot was extended during the war and reconstructed in the 1950s, but there had never been any office facilities, and it was demolished in 1962, buses having to park out in the open. This photograph taken in 1964 shows two Lodekkas, a Leyland TS8 and a PS1 parked early one icy March morning. When Longtown reopened in 1967, the Gretna duties were transferred to it and the garage there closed. It was a basic shed at Canberra Road, capable of accommodating four single deckers, and had been in use since 1933. The original proposal in 1957 had been to build a new depot at Gretna replacing Longtown, and land was eventually purchased in 1962, but there were planning problems and the land was later sold off. The number of buses parked overnight at Longtown gradually reduced and by 1983 there were only two Leopards, The empty space was used for storing buses, but there continued to be a sleeper kept at Langholm. Carlisle depot itself closed in October 1981, with the remaining eleven buses being garaged in the Ribble premises at Willowholme Road, and Longtown depot finally closed in 1983.

When Caledonian took over the services of Andrew Harper of Peebles in January 1932, they acquired the licence for their service from Dumfries to Edinburgh via Biggar first started by Dickson of Kirkpatrick Durham. Space for one bus was rented at Central Garage, Biggar and at the Roseburn Garage in Edinburgh, supplemented by space at a newly-built garage in Gorgie Road. When Western absorbed Caledonian in January 1950, SMT took over the Edinburgh services, parking up to four buses overnight at Western's garage in Dumfries, and two at their own in Biggar. The Dumfries based buses were required to operate the routes to Edinburgh via Biggar and Moffat, weekend and summer duplicates on the Biggar service, and from Summer 1955, a Friday only service from Dumfries to Selkirk This arrangement continued until 31st May 1964 when Western buses first appeared at weekends on duplicates and the Moffat service. From 22 May 1965, a Western bus alternated with Eastern Scottish on the Biggar service, where a bus was garaged overnight, and on 19th June 1974 it was the Western bus, WSD750K (DL2359), one of four Leopards allocated new to Dumfries in 1972, and the regular vehicle allocated. It is about to leave the depot for the 7.35 am service into Edinburgh with Eastern Scottish Bedford YRQ ZC451A running light to West Linton for the 7.45 am duplicate.

The Carlisle bus outstationed at Langholm ran into Carlisle, and the regular vehicle during the early sixties was Guy LUF MSD412 (DG1548) although in the winter when that road could be difficult in snow and ice, Alexander bodied Leyland PS1 CSD9 (DL603) was preferred. By 1964, Lodekka DB1632 had become the regular allocation, and when Carlisle depot closed, 53 seat Leopard OSJ615R (DL2615) was kept there. However, Western also operated to Langholm from Lockerbie via Waterbeck on Saturdays and Sundays, and from Annan via Canonbie on weekdays. With only two runs daily along quiet rural roads, this was a light duty and the regular performer was Leyland TS7 DL51 featured earlier. However, CSD22 (DL616) had arrived at Annan depot in 1963, having been transferred from Greenock to Dumfries two years previously. Already fifteen years old, it only had three months left in service when photographed near Canonbie in June 1965, being sold to a contractor based in St. Helens. It was replaced on the Langholm service by one of two Bristol MW6Gs at Annan depot already converted for OMO operation, TCS157-8 (DT1709-10), but the service was finally withdrawn in April 1983.

In Dumfries and Galloway, in the early sixties, there were still elderly Leylands to be seen which were no longer in service. In Annan, VD3489 owned by Crombie Construction was parked on waste ground in February 1963, having been withdrawn from service with Western in December 1958. It was new to Central SMT in 1934, one of a batch of 110 Leyland Lion LT5As with 32 seat rear entrance all-metal Leyland bodies. These bodies proved troublesome and required remedial attention within a couple of years. In 1946, Western was looking for suitable second hand chassis to re-body in order to reinstate its premier Glasgow to London service, and acquired 20 of this batch from Central SMT and ten further Lions from other sources. All were fitted with Leyland 7.4 litre engines as used on the new PS1 model, and they received 30 seat Brush coach bodies. However, when replaced on the London service by new Burlingham bodied Leyland PS1s in 1948-9, seven were immediately sold and the remainder reseated with 35 bus seats, and had their sliding doors replaced by folding ones. Now downgraded to service work and private hires, their black and white colours were exchanged for red bus livery, and they survived for another ten years. VD3489 became IL31 when fleet numbering was introduced, and after leaving Kilmarnock depot when replaced on the London rota, operated out of Inchinnan depot until withdrawn.

Further West in the village of Creetown was parked Leyland Cheetah, LZ2A WG7516, operated by Solway Precast and owned by a distant relative of mine. Withdrawn by Alexanders in January 1959, it had been sold to a dealer in Chesterfield and purchased by Sowerby's Tours of Gilsland who operated staff transport to the MOD research centre at Spadeadam, passing to this operator in 1961. It was new in June 1939 as one of 50 dual purpose vehicles with Alexander bodies able to accommodate 39 passengers because the engines protruded into the saloon being covered with a cowl. With six cylinder petrol engines they were underpowered due to the weight of the metal-framed body, particularly with a full load of passengers, and these were replaced with 7.4 litre oil engines after the war. The chassis did not allow for a luggage boot, and so a return was made to a roof rack, although WG7516 has had its removed as was common practice in later life. The original half drop windows have been replaced by sliding vents, and the glass louvres above the windows gone, producing a rather austere appearance compared with its original elegant looks. Operating out of Arbroath depot in its later years, it was little used and would have been a good second hand purchase.

Alexander's Leyland Cheetahs were a popular purchase from dealers, even although many were twenty years old. Clark of Glencaple ran WG7628 between 1958 and 1960. Leith of Sanquhar acquired three and used them intensively. All had operated in the Northern region of Alexanders and were purchased from the dealer Millburn Motors in Glasgow. WG7508, which donated the rear portion of its body to Crossley KSM40, had operated out of Montrose depot, and ran for five years before being cannibalised. WG7514 had been withdrawn at Stonehaven depot in February 1958, arriving at Sanquhar in October 1957. It was withdrawn in 1963 and derelict in July 1965 when I photographed WG7620 converted into a Tow Wagon. It was allocated to MacDuff depot and withdrawn in September 1968, but did not reach Millburn Motors until April 1959. It was still in service in 1963, but appeared in its new role in March 1964, surviving until 1967 when at the age of 28 it was also scrapped. Parked beside it is Leith's latest double decker DRN280.

Leith's all Leyland PD2 was near the end of its life when I photographed Gibson's PD2/20 LFS405 at the Whitesands in March 1971, the pair being the only Leyland PD2s running in the Dumfries area at that time. One of 100 new to Edinburgh Corporation in 1954 with ultra light Metro-Cammell 60 seat bodies, it was reseated to 62 in 1959. Among the first of this batch to be sold, it was disposed of in September 1970 to the dealer Irvine (Tiger Coaches) of Salsburgh where it was fitted with a rear door. It was acquired by Gibson in November of that year, replacing a Northern Counties Guy Arab IV (RTC699) and was their sole double decker, running until December 1974 when it was replaced by a Leyland PS1 re-bodied as a double decker for Barton Transport by Northern Counties with a 63 seat front entrance body (798BAL) such was the variety in the Gibson fleet. LFS405 was sold back to Tiger Coaches, and passed to a private owner.

Former Ribble all Leyland PD2s were popular purchases for independent operators, and in addition to the unique Motor Show exhibit with a Burlingham body and a PD1 engine (CCK636) Carruthers operated two from the same batch of 50 Leyland PD2/3s as Leith. New in 1950, DRN241-90 (1301-50) had 53 seats and hand-operated doors, and initially operated long distance and premium Ribble routes such as that traversing the Lake District on service from Lancaster to Keswick. DRN249, photographed at the Whitesands in May 1965, was sold to the dealer Cowley of Salford in February 1964, passing on to the Preston branch of Millburn Motors and to Carruthers in June acquiring fleet number 1. It ran until May 1968 and was sold to the headquarters of Millburn Motors in Glasgow. Until 1969 Carruthers usually had a couple of double deckers on the road at any one time, and DRN264 had arrived at the same time being allocated number 8. In contrast, when withdrawn in August 1968, it saw further service with the contractor Palmer of Kilwinning until 1970. Parked beside DRN249 is Gibson's former demonstrator, all Leyland PD2 MTA747 with a highbridge body.

Another Carruthers vehicle which had been exhibited at a motor show was a unique Atkinson built in 1957 on a modified forward control lorry chassis with a 37 seat Plaxton body as a demonstrator for Ceylon. Two other longer chassis were constructed at the Atkinson factory at Walton-le-Dale near Preston, and fitted with 41 seat Roe bodies for Sunderland Corporation. With a chassis classified as L644LWL, the Plaxton bodied Atkinson had a 4 cylinder Gardner engine, and was registered NHL127 by the dealer Comberhill Motors of Wakefield. After a further period as a demonstrator, it was acquired by Simpson of Rosehearty in 1960, moving on to Calder of Dunphail in April 1962, then nearby Fraser of Forres in November 1964, before going to a dealer, this time Millburn Motors in Glasgow. Returning north, it passed to Clan Garage at Kyle of Lochalsh and back south to Carruthers by September 1965. Within two years it was off on its travels again via Millburn Motors up the coast to Garelochhead Coaches in January 1968, back to Millburn Motors in September, and finally back up to the north east to a contractor at Aberdeen, and was last seen in The Black Isle in 1971. Despite its obvious unpopularity, this unique bus operated on rural roads all over Scotland for a creditable 15 years.

The more usual second hand acquisition for Carruthers was the Bedford VAS, and SRS134 (fleet no.12) arrived from Alexander (Northern) in August 1972. Ten years previously, the Alexander companies, newly-formed after the empire was divided into Northern, Midland and Fife in 1961, each introduced one with a 30 seat Duple Midland body to assess the use of such a vehicle in a fleet where there were only full sized service buses. This was not a success and only Northern bought one further example. SRS134 (NW264), new in May 1962, started life at Huntly depot operating a network of OMO services along quiet, narrow Aberdeenshire roads, replacing a Bedford OB. Three years later when Strachans were taken over, it moved to their former depot at Ballater to operate a school contract for pupils at Crathie Primary School. No further use was found for it by 1971 and after storage it was sold. Carruthers acquired it in August 1972 and after four years sold it to a local building contractor in Dumfries. It was photographed in July 1974 beside their premises at New Abbey.

A popular source for Bedfords for the Carruthers fleet was the former MacBrayne vehicles acquired by Highland Omnibuses, and in June 1977 375FGB (12) arrived via the usual source, the dealer S&N Motors. A Bedford VAS1 with a 29 seat Duple body, it was one of eight bought in 1962 for extended tours throughout the islands, passing to Highland Omnibuses in September 1970 as their CD43. Initially based in Stornoway, it had been operating in Harris when Highland acquired it, and was moved to Skye where it spent the next six years on tours, private hires and school contracts. Carruthers operated it for three years and sold it to the dealer Moseley in Coatbridge, and while there was the possibility of it being preserved, it ended up as a car transporter. Parked beside it on the Whitesands is 52 seat Willowbrook bodied Ford RJS192L new to Newton of Dingwall, one of three acquired with high seating capacities, SJS36L with 56 seats replacing the last double decker.

Haugh of Castle Douglas, a family firm which only briefly operated a service run, but started in 1890 and introduced charabancs for excursions and tours in 1916, still trades today as a Vauxhall dealer with garages in Castle Douglas and Dumfries. Licenses were also held for church services from Castle Douglas and Gelston to Kelton Church until 1966, school services, and briefly the service run from Castle Douglas to Tongland from 1951. Three buses were still operated in 1964. SW7990 was an Austin K4 with a Mann Egerton 31 seat coach body new to the company in 1949. HXX633 was a Bedford OB with a 27 seat Duple body first licensed to Bradshaw's Super Coaches of London in November 1946. They were photographed at the Crown Garage in Castle Douglas. The third vehicle was KVD828, a Bedford SBG with a Duple 36 seat body with a 'butterfly' grille new to Peter Irvine of Salsburgh in 1955, acquired by Haugh in 1961 as its fifth owner, and outshopped in a pale blue and grey livery.

Another elderly Bedford still operating in 1964 was WG9918, an OWB new to Alexander (W137) in 1943 with a utility SMT 32 seat body to Duple design. The chassis alone was sold to the dealer Millburn Motors in August 1948, and the operator R.Murray & Sons of Stranraer acquired it with this 29 seat Duple body. While of contemporary design, the possibility exists that this was a second-hand body, but no obvious source for it has been discovered. It was photographed at their depot at Stranraer beside LVD262, a Leyland Tiger Cub new to Hutchison of Overtown in 1955 with a 41 seat Alexander body (together with LVD263 on page 4 acquired by Carruthers) acquired in 1958. Both were withdrawn in December 1965 when Western acquired the company, but none of the vehicles, nor their West End garage. WG9918 was sold to another dealer in Glasgow, and LVD262 passed to Aberfoyle Motors and ultimately McLennan of Spittalfield. The services which Western inherited included Stranraer town services, the Drummore route on which Caledonian had previously operated, and a network of services to surrounding villages, giving Western at last a monopoly in the area.

By September 1972 when this photograph was taken at Stranraer depot, Western still exercised a complete monopoly in Galloway and the Machars. The left half of the depot which had been rented to Caledonian Road Services since 1949 had just been vacated. Later, the implementation of OMO would be completed in early 1977, and the depot receive its own code of S (and Carlisle designated E) in June 1977, when it received separate status and its own district traffic superintendent. Just arrived from Dumfries is Bristol RELH6G DSD712D (DT2071) which had a different history to 2072 seen on page 12 in that it (with 2070) was converted again in 1974 to a 41 seater, and lent to Alexander Northern as back up for the four (2076-8/184 reverted to 38 seat toilet coaches) already there for the Aberdeen to London service. It did not return until December 1976, to Kirkcudbright depot, painted in red and cream livery and with 45 seats again. All of 2070-4 were withdrawn in July 1980 and scrapped by dealers. When the Dumfries to Stranraer railway line was closed in June 1965, an express service was introduced, running three times a day from Dumfries Railway Station, and year old Leopards XCS921-2 (1900-1) were transferred from Inchinnan depot to operate it, but it was taken off in 1971, and the timetable simplified.

It wasn't until March 1977 that all of the remaining former Bristol London toilet coaches had arrived in the Dumfries area, all now in red and cream colours and with 45 seats, the capacity being determined by the regulation that above this number, an additional nearside emergency exit would be required. One, however, DSD718D was fitted with 53 bus seats in 1978 and required this additional exit. The two transferred to Highland Omnibuses in June 1971 (DSD701-2D) were returned in July 1978, now numbered DT2701-2 and visibly altered as seen in this photograph of 2702 (DSD 702D) at Whitesands in October. They were also converted but in Inverness, with 49 second hand coach seats from Bedford VAS and Albion Vikings respectively. Acquired for the Inverness to Ullapool service, they were initially used on tours. DSD702D was not converted until September 1972, and the pair were normally allocated to the Inverness to Edinburgh and Glasgow services, being the most reliable and fast vehicles available. Parked beside are DT2065, now at Penpont depot waiting to return to Thornhill, and DT2068 just in from Annan. Both had previously spent three years at Inchinnan depot on Scotia Tours with 41 recliner seats before the further conversion to 45 seats and repainting into red and cream prior to coming south.

Not only had Dumfries depot been allocated the first (and only) Bristol FL6Gs entering the Western fleet, but the first two FLF6Gs also came to Dumfries, and the four were the only 30 feet Lodekkas ever to operate in the area. All were 70 seaters with the uprated Gardner 6LX engine, and when TCS159-60 (DB1711-2) arrived in June 1962, fifteen months after the FL6Gs, the quartet remained in the area, until DB1711-2 were transferred to Johnstone depot nine years later and replaced by Daimler Fleetlines converted for OMO operation. They spent the entire time on Dumfries town services, principally from Lincluden to Locharbriggs, but on summer weekends would often run to Gatehouse of Fleet on Saturdays or even to Stranraer. Between 1964 and 1966, one would often be the Castle Douglas sleeper when passenger numbers exceeded the capacity of 60 seater RAG403 (DB1637.) However, DB1711, photographed on the Whitesands in September 1962, had actually been on the service to Lochside. Both were delicensed in May 1978 and sold to dealers for scrap. However, DB1711 had a short reprieve, being loaned to Greenock and on to Central SMT from August to November 1978.

Although the first Daimler Fleetline was not allocated to the Dumfries area until September 1970 when GCS170E (DR2117) arrived from Kilmarnock, Cumnock Fleetlines had visited Dumfries on the service from Glasgow since December 1967 when JAG524-9F (CR2171-6) arrived new and were allocated to this lengthy service. Parked at the Whitesands in June 1968, CR2173, a 75 seat Alexander bodied model with a Gardner 6LX engine, is screened for the 9.30 pm short working to Auchinleck to return to its home depot. It was converted for OMO operation the following year and later transferred to Stranraer depot in February 1984, completing exactly 20 years in service. Parked beside it is Carruthers Bedford OB KGN433 (fleet number 9), new in May 1949 with a Duple 29 seat bus body, acquired from the Metropolitan Police in 1963. Identical JXT483 (number 3) had come from the same source a year earlier, and both were withdrawn in 1969, JXT483 going for scrap. KGN433, however, passed through the hands of several preservationists, now being with Blue Motors of Blackpool.

The family business of Campbell of Gatehouse of Fleet had its origins in the nineteenth century and continued to operate local bus services until its last remaining one from Kirkcudbright to Gatehouse via Borgue ceased on March 31st 1965. Western SMT introduced a replacement service between Kirkcudbright and Borgue with two return journeys and additional runs on a Wednesday and Saturday. Initially this was operated by a full size vehicle, a five year old 41 seat dual purpose Alexander bodied Guy LUF as seen on page 12. This was replaced three years later by a 49 seat Leyland Leopard AAG96B (DL1894) still in coach livery which was Kirkcudbright depot's first 36 feet long vehicle and first OMO operated bus. The Bedford OB (SW7449) which was regularly used on the service was new to Campbell in 1950 with a 29 seat Duple body, and one of only four vehicles in the fleet when it ceased trading. It was photographed at Kirkcudbright in 1964.